Cleaving the Clouds

Cleaving the Clouds

Poems by

Margaret Anne Kean

© 2023 Margaret Anne Kean. All rights reserved.
This material may not be reproduced in any form, published,
reprinted, recorded, performed, broadcast,
rewritten or redistributed without
the explicit permission of Margaret Anne Kean.
All such actions are strictly prohibited by law.

Cover image by David Mark, "Fields and Cloud," via Pixabay
Cover design by Shay Culligan
Author photo by Chris Flynn

ISBN: 978-1-63980-459-7

Kelsay Books
502 South 1040 East, A-119
American Fork, Utah 84003
Kelsaybooks.com

For my parents

Elene Ruth Roussey Hawthorne
April 8, 1927–December 3, 2020
&
Donald Claire Hawthorne
May 1, 1925–December 30, 2020

Acknowledgments

Grateful acknowledgement is extended to the editors of the following journals in which these poems first appeared, sometimes in earlier versions:

Anti-Heroin Chic: "Mom's Last CT Scan," "Hospice"

EcoTheo Review: "Against This Drought"

Eunoia Review: "The Flow of Tides," "Mom's Body in Freefall"

poems-for-all.com: "A Candle for My Father"

San Antonio Review: "Last Rites," "A Lament Rises from the Nursing Home," "The Faded Calendar," "Rage-Reading Einstein After My Parents Died 27 Days Apart"

Contents

Among High-Rises in Downtown Los Angeles	13
Mom's Last CT Scan	14
I've Never Thought Much About White Noise	16
Hospice	17
Mom's Body in Freefall	18
Last Rites	19
The Three-Piece Suit	20
The Hummingbird	21
Buried Cities	22
At the Retirement Community	
I Ask My Father to Whistle	25
A Candle for My Father on His 95th Birthday	26
A Lament Rises from the Nursing Home	27
The Faded Calendar	28
Ode to My Father	29
Social Distancing	30
Conducting Vivaldi's Violin Concerto	
in A Minor on the Way Home from Work	31
Coyote Call at Sunrise	32
Rage-Reading Einstein	
After My Parents Died 27 Days Apart	35
At the Art Gallery After the Pandemic	38
How Long Will I Hold My Breath?	39
Against This Drought	40
Dissolving	43
Beyond the Curtain	44
The Flow of Tides	45
Mothers and Daughters	46
Elene Ruth	47
Grief Work	49
Ursa Hangs Low in the Winter Sky	50

A monarch flits above the grasses, looks for a place to land.

Compost must thaw before being stirred into the garden.

Among High-Rises in Downtown Los Angeles

Mozart strides out of the Colburn School on Grand Avenue,
        blue frock coat over tan breeches,
buckles shining, brown hair tied at the neck.

A white cockatoo holds court at dinner
        atop a white chair outside Mexicali café.

Our Lady of the Angels cathedral bells toll the seventh hour,
        my phone echoes—

    All the tumors grew seven millimeters,
        my mother cries.

    The raptor's claws grip
the padded gauntlet of his handler at Second and Hope

while under the guardian lion's statue in Chinatown,
        I shake my head slowly, try to steady my stomach.

    What does seven millimeters look like inside a lung?
How many more millimeters are left for breath?

Nearby, a man madly twirls his bike around the intersection
        one leg extended backward, right hand pointed to the sky.

    Mozart has disappeared around the corner.
Will the handler give the word that releases the raptor?

Mom's Last CT Scan

Everything is backwards, horizontal slices
flipped: on the right monitor her left lung
fills with lesions that show white,

airways, black. Liquid, like two grey half-moons
inside each lung, invades soft darkness.
There is nothing soft

about severing—
as her results filled the screen
threads to our future were cut.

*

Her darkness shrinks each month.
White expands against her chest wall
close to the rib where I once rested
newly tied to her breathing,
the strong beat of her heart.

*

Today, a film seems to cover the sun,
our two bodies submerged in shadow.

Today, it seems we must speak in gentle voices,
talk of death on familiar terms, like someone

who suddenly finds alarms irrelevant,
has no need to scrub the sink.

*

I need to shout about living—the roses
on her patio and the stories she has yet to tell;
about her home where she will die,

the vacancies opening in my life,
about the months of Saturdays
at her table, paying her bills.

        *

My eyes paid
the darkness
last night,
tears pooling

on cheek bones,
saturating skin:
that thin membrane
that once separated

me from her raw
bone and blood,
from the hollow
inside, where I

want to hide again.
But the light
inside her
is pushing me out.

I've Never Thought Much About White Noise

but today it started buzzing
in my head, a constant static.

I yearn for quiet
but grief keeps interrupting.

If only it was possible to capture it,
compress it into threads,

weave them like a magician
weaves flames with her fingers

then settles the fiery pattern into water
with a hiss and a sigh.

Hospice

If I place my feet on the floor
      I will walk into this day.

If I open my eyes
      I will see her hands:

gravity sucking water out of skin,
      collapsing cancer-riddled bones.

I wish I were night leaning down
      to touch her eyes closed:

in her bedroom I smell loneliness
      on father's frayed wool bathrobe:

the one she's worn since his fall.

Mom's Body in Freefall

Freed of land's constraints, her river
is falling over the cliff, spreading out

catching light
in its droplets
as it speeds downward.

All that has held us
      together
            pours over.

Under the roaring,
my voice rages
against rocks.

I must become an anvil
as the weight bears down.

Last Rites

Black face masks litter the schoolyard
like fallen baby crows crushed underfoot:
cries silenced, hearts stopped.

Mom's thirst for air called out one last time,
desire and pain issued from her open mouth
leaving my tongue crumbled on the ground.

My throat aches, in need of anointing.
Leave the sacred oil off her eyes, her forehead.
Pour it instead down my darkened tunnel,

coat the wailing that rises against the tightness,
                        words stuck,
opening clamped, airways thick with loss.

The Three-Piece Suit

At 3:30 in the morning the mortician shrugged into the jacket
    of his three-piece navy-blue suit as he stepped from the van.
As though his suit made her death more palatable. As though
    the sheet he wrapped around her body could sanitize us
from feeling. The covering of her face took our breath away.

Can we stop surrounding death with a black border?
    It doesn't require black tie or even business attire.
Leave off make-up that hides swollen eyes.
    The body releases fluid. Yes, I'm crying.
Yes, she soiled the diaper.

Farewell sweet one, the cards say. But her breath as she lay dying
    was anything but sweet. Muscles atrophied and sagging
under skin that wrinkled as it fell away. Her stomach finally
    flattened out, hip bones prominent. Her heart raced,
weakened each hour. Her last cry raised her up, then stillness.

We scrape away grief that litters our path, like leaves we rake
    off asphalt, tuck into dustbins, put out on the street
for pickup. I look at leaf piles now and think of her
    return to earth. Move my feet through fiery purple and red,
gold and shades of brown.

The Hummingbird

another victim to the clear glass
soft underbelly exposed on the porch tiles

grey and green fluff under which its heart beats fast
kneeling close I startle to hear my voice—*oh sweetheart*

        I'm so sorry

        I longed to touch but

I feared to stroke the little body
after Mom's heart stopped

I couldn't bear to clean her prepare her for burial
my mind splintered

        would touch calm this heart

this pulsing these convulsions
its eye moved back and forth

rocking perhaps wary perhaps
trying to figure how to get away perhaps

        grasp how we arrived

curled on the cold tile only temporarily together my eyes moved
rapidly disconnected again why does thinking shudder away

        into emptiness

when the bird is fallen

        body broken

Buried Cities

There are buried cities/one beneath the other.
—Mark Doty

She lay down first. Hands fallen at her side.
On top of her open mouth I blew a kiss,
lay the foundation for the next.

Layers upon layers we bury them.
Bodies stacked for archeologists to find
when this civilization has disintegrated.

How deep will they have to dig?
Will they read the signs properly
like one reads rings on a tree?

      Seven lean years
followed by seven fat ones.

She had many buried cities inside her.
Only four were ever excavated.
The rest died with her.

Blown away on her last breath.

The song of the finches sweetens the air.

He walked under the canopy of song.

At the Retirement Community
I Ask My Father to Whistle

after Li-Young Lee's "I Ask My Mother to Sing"

     —and Broadway tunes break out,
flow into operatic arias.

Inhaling,
his cheeks shape the air into carillon bells

that ring clear and strong
as they have since I was a child.

I loop my arm through his. As we walk,
he leans, and whistles: windows fly open in welcome,

the Whistler's notes soar through screen doors,
wriggle into sidewalk cracks,

flow underneath shrubs, join
with bubbles from koi swimming

in the pond under the wooden bridge
and in the kitchen are kneaded

into bread dough
that waits to rise.

A Candle for My Father on His 95th Birthday

A private man, a banked fire.

Once, we leaned against his warmth.
His light refracted through us, sparks enlivened,

light catching light, leaping candle to candle,
dispersing across the land, darkness dissipated

by the glow of a thousand flames, like fireflies
fill the summer night.

But now in his winter his fuel
runs low,

starter fire
scattered,

dimming
to the muted

sound

of a

single

dying

ember.

A Lament Rises from the Nursing Home

My father is unshaven as though he just woke—
grey stubble on bruised skin.

What time is it? he asks. *It's 3 pm,* I answer.
Shouldn't I be asleep? he asks.

His eyes opaque, search mine,
seek something I cannot provide.

A shadow covers his brain, the one that once knew
Greek and Latin unable now to hold

five minutes of English.
I want to go home, he says. *Why can't I go home?*

His day has turned into night. Night confuses him.
I hold his hand and stroke his bony back.

The Faded Calendar

An old boat house in Maine on Lake Androscoggin.
A summer day in the 1930s. Two skinny boys. Brothers.

Curious, they rowed under the lake door of the abandoned home.
Inside they climbed up stairs from the water to the landing.

One page from an old monthly calendar remained
tacked to the wall: January 1888.

Kept on his bookshelf for decades after,
its lamination crinkled, brown with age.

His brother gone now. The story faded.
His mind as well.

Two things were stolen during his life:
he took only one.

Ode to My Father

A prophet, tall in his black robe
preaching from the pulpit,

the man who wrote limericks
and conducted Mozart concertos at dinner.

Laughter was never far from his eyes,
his mouth puckered to whistle or jest.

Now his grizzled mouth wraps grotesquely
around spoons, attempts to capture

slippery strawberries, family names. Eyes that saw
the hearts of his children now wander vacant,

his mind like a string that has no beginning
or end, just a loop of emptiness.

Where is the voice that rose and fell in cadence,
that led me out of the desert of self-doubt,

lifted by the warmth of his words,
the breeze of his mirth?

The prophet needs a diaper change,
the preacher needs a bib.

Social Distancing

Parrots protest
my presence, as my feet crunch
over loose asphalt
under their tree. Their voices
cut through air like the ratcheting
coughs of my father.

I'm not allowed to visit.
Everywhere—the disease
of distance: streets eerily
quiet as we hide
from the breath of our neighbors.
Bodies we love
quarantined behind glass.
Dad's memories, unreachable.
Time warped, frozen
by untouched skin.

Conducting Vivaldi's Violin Concerto
in A Minor on the Way Home from Work

Dad conducted everywhere: at dinner, on vacation,
from his seat at concerts. Brown eyes sparking

with intense concentration, his whole body engaged
as Brahms' Hungarian Dance #5

or Chopin's Nocturne Opus 9 spun
on the turn table in the living room.

Or when we begged him to play opening chords
of Rachmaninoff's Prelude in G Minor on our upright.

In the car, the soaring line of Vivaldi's melody
broke through my fatigue. I started conducting.

The movement of my arms conjured an image of his hands:
dark skin, black hair, crooked middle fingers

(just like Grandpa's, just like mine), college ring
on one hand, wedding ring on the other.

As my arms moved in 4/4 time, the vibration
of a dirge droned throughout my body.

At his deathbed, dressed in full PPE, I had opened my phone
to classical music, hoped his hearing still functioned

even though he couldn't conduct
or open his eyes to say goodbye.

I played Bach's Brandenburg Concertos as tears sped down,
completely out of rhythm with the orderly march.

I let the orchestra speak our language,
accompany him through his final measures.

Coyote Call at Sunrise

A lone coyote threw its head back and howled.
The thrust of his throat, primordial.

I wanted to respond with something urgent,
perhaps my own howl.

The coyote bent its head back a second time
pointed nose to widening sky.

Begun in the belly, the long cry shivered the dawn—
my agony met his in mid-air.

Lightning convulsed horizontally,

cleaved the clouds. Hail fell rapidly

as though it too felt urgency—

damascened the ground

in layers of white nubble

before disappearing at moonrise.

Rage-Reading Einstein
After My Parents Died 27 Days Apart

If each moment encompasses all time—

    let me lose the constraint of this body

        let me leap into the galaxy

    cross dimensions as an astronaut blasts

through earth's atmosphere

    or an ant crosses the shortened string.

        Let me bend the time-space continuum

    cut the tether that ties me inside my skin

and touch their hands once again.

    I want to co-exist within other worlds

        that flash in the corners of my eyes,

    mingle with molecules that shift

to make space for unseen density.

    Lately, I've been looking into the night sky, searching

        for two new stars born of gas and dust.

    Maybe one day my core will become hot enough

to ignite fusion and I'll be reborn too,

    my leftover particles tumbling across the universe

        as dust to dust I return.

    Light from distant stars takes time to travel—

I see their light within my darkness

    but they are always there, always have been,

        like the lost, our dead. Like fog around a streetlamp,

    death covers their light only momentarily.

In December, within the nanosecond between the light leaving

    their eyes to touch my face,

        they changed. Everything changed.

    I want to breathe again within that nanosecond

to inhale the gaze that escaped that day. And yet . . .

    here I stand, feet solidly on the earth,

        while all around me centuries of sorrow

    swirl throughout the firmament

and black holes swallow stars within the whole

    of a single breath.

        This morning I shook my fists at G-d—

    not because of death,

but because gravity is heavier

    than my imagination or star dust.

At the Art Gallery After the Pandemic

Still enveloped in a fog, sight blurry
like these impressionist paintings,

we keep looking for figures amid the colors.
But all is obscured, veiled, as though bodies dissolved

into paint, were stirred and brushed onto a canvas stretched
inside a frame the world wants to leave in a museum,

                                     a plaque to its right:
"When Everything Spun Out of Control."

Hidden under the brush strokes are a million lives
reduced to this 20' x 23' painting.

How can birds still sing?
Why doesn't the sky rip and tear itself with mourning?

Standing in front of Manet's *Rochefort's Escape,*
I know my anchors lie at the bottom of that ocean.

If I were to step into the boat, the water would churn,
like clouds in Van Gogh's *Starry Night.*

If I fell in, would I survive?
Would bones and blood blend with the ocean bottom,

or would air reach me before my body
joined the swirling blues and greens.

How Long Will I Hold My Breath?

This wind that defines my shape,
        that supports cells that hold me upright
as they did when I floated
        in the high school pool
learning the mystery that separates me
        from liquid that threatens to drown.

This same air that makes me kin
        to brightly feathered, squawking parrots
whose wings rapidly carry them through sky
        not unlike bats that flicker through night,
black and white versions of the fireworks
        over the canyon that light the darkness

then dissipate into smokiness inside lungs
        that will sustain this body
until I'm released from their rhythm:
        the final exhalation that weighs nothing
but carries much.
        That casts only a shadow on the slate walkways.

Against This Drought

white flesh of the ripe red anjou
        its sweet juice leaks onto the plate

salt on the zucchini leaches water

drought deprives our skin: removed my parents' touch

we crave what escapes

the gingko tree at the childhood home brought us back:
        its burnished leaves, thickened trunk

we poured their ashes, some beach sand,
        sugared the earth

            *

we're no longer virgins to death

yet still unable to gauge the distance
the moment of its arrival

unable to look directly
unable to look away

suspended—
                out of present time

like the birder who listens
blind in the dark, unmoving,

anticipating the owl's call

we're drawn to the chasm now before us
its magnetic pull

yet we wait

at the train station
at the movie theater
at the racetrack

we wait

at the coffee shop
at the drugstore
at the restaurant

we wait

but we can't watch
this other meal being prepared

the heart beats again

this time

                *

when words no longer suffice

when tongues thirst for what they cannot taste

our voices become trombones

throbbing down the scale like Etta James

dry thunder roils the night sky

even the plumbing of the old house moans

untamed ferocity

against the impossibility of our yearning

against this drought we remove anonymous grass

we plant purple smoke bush next to olive shrubs

and crawling manzanita, pulled back to the first task of creation

we become proximate, a familiar to heaven's breath,

the Japanese elm and mockingbirds

perhaps this is what we seek:

to be called

by name

Dissolving

Cells align to form a leg,
feet to fill sneakers,
a hand to hold paper,
another to hold a paintbrush.

Nightfall brings dissolving.

As eyes shutter and breathing slows,
we segue into dreams,
transition,
then pirouette into bendable time,

let go the discipline of formation.

Beyond the Curtain

Perhaps it's the way the smell of eucalyptus trees and fog
      pulls memory into her lungs.
Or the way her fingers automatically sort scree
      as if knowing their touch can unlock
the mystery of the mountain. Or the way
      the black Labrador cocks his ears toward empty space
as though he hears something move.
      Perhaps it was hearing her mother's voice speak her name
in a dream exactly one week following the passing.
      Upon waking, the air still suffused with warmth,
she wonders yet again about time and space
      and who else shares this air she breathes.
Can the invisible curtain separating us be ripped?
      How impenetrable this secret seems.
How elusive the knowing.
      Evening is the time for ferocious tenderness,
when barriers become thinnest, as at Beltane
      when gods and faerie are said to traverse the rippled veil.
Perhaps if she listens hard enough to the silence of the night,
      she can find and touch its edges.
Come closer to flickering flames
      she senses burn inside, around and beyond her.
Are there truly angels? Jacob wrestled with one.

The Flow of Tides

Inside the cove, the San Francisco Bay pulls back again,
        morning fog envelops surrounding foothills.
Ruins of rusted ship parts stick out of wet sand,

remnants from a Gold Rush shipwreck: a lost anchor,
        cracked rudder, hull broken and corroded.
From a distance, one bent piece could be a man kneeling,

frozen in supplication. Every morning
        he reappears with the receding tide,
not unlike memories that resurface often,

strangely intact, perhaps softened by the flow of tides.
        Two egrets stroll past, long legs lift carefully,
find sustenance in exposed silt.

Mothers and Daughters

Mom was a lion stalking her prey.
Purpose etched in the movement of every muscle.
I followed, a jack rabbit,
leaping over cracks in the sidewalks,
scrambling over debris,
hungry to show her my strength.

Today, on the dirt path into the national forest,
I walk deliberately. I've learned to listen,
to raise my eyes to watch a woodpecker,
its red head rat-a-tat-tatting against the tree.
To be still and patient enough
to catch the entire flock returning,
dozens descending onto branches
that still offer bounty
although riddled with holes.

The stream braids itself over the rocks
and gains strength.
The hound dog moves fearlessly
across the forest bed,
bounds over boulders in the stream
to race up and down
the far side of the water.

I hear steps behind me.
Look back.
Maybe I will wait.
Let my daughters catch up
before I reach the waterfall.

Ask them to belay me up its slippery slope.

Elene Ruth

Odd items she used to order still pop up
when I shop online: Mocha Mix and Bran,

Gelato and Canned Salmon. Scarves she started to knit
were finished by her friend, leftover yarn given to another.

Since her death, I've sent hundreds
of black and white photos to be captured by cameras:

pixels placed into the ether:
her childhood in liminal space, just out of reach.

She has joined our ancestors,
those solemn faces in front of heavy drapery,

buttoned boots poking out under long skirts
that must have dragged on dirt roads, covering legs

that bore children who became our elders. Generations
held together within air we can't breathe.

Always at a distance. Unlike the years when her blue eyes
and petite frame fit under my chin.

Covered by a pink nightgown, her tiny body
was incinerated in the crematorium,

the port for cancer-fighting chemicals melted
into her bones. Knuckles, grown large with arthritis,

no longer troubled. Lungs no longer struggling for air.
All of who she was—gone. Only fragments left.

Perhaps I'll write her an ode: a response to a portrait
by the Old Masters she studied so vigorously.

Show her I listened
as she toured me through museums.

But I'll probably slip outside and find a way
to pull in the raucous call of the crows,

put a peacock in the corner of the painting,
to her surprise.

Grief Work

Sharpened by death,
an axe furiously
splits wood for flames.
But splinters spear my heart
and warmth slips further away.

    *

Under the myrtle
dew drops rest on purple leaves.
I pause my pacing.
Reflecting light, they hold me,
for one still moment.

    *

Squirrel on the wire
twitches its tail for balance,
leaps into the embrace
of the pine tree—confident
it can cross all divides.

Ursa Hangs Low in the Winter Sky

I hibernated with bears in my dreams last night,
under the rich loam of sleep, heavy clouds and barren trees.

Resting in the kindness of their quiet,
absence transformed into intimacy.

I still feel our kindred's presence
although their bodies are no longer within reach,

unlike the warm fur that cuddled me through the night,
the long slow breaths and eased hearts.

In the morning's post-storm air, I stand alone
and remember their smell,

not cinnamon, more earthy,
pine and redwood-mulched and dirt-drenched

like a scented candle that tries to re-create
the illusion of woods.

Maybe today I can exhale grief without using words.
Unwrap my fingers from the gift of sorrow.

Maybe it doesn't require a tight grip anymore
like a light touch on the clutch moves a car into another gear.

Tonight, under a warm blanket, I will again twist the kaleidoscope.
Watch as colors move and fall into another shape.

About the Author

Margaret Anne Kean was born in Los Angeles and raised in Southern California. She received her BA in British/American Literature from Scripps College and, after raising her family, received her MFA in Creative Writing/Poetry from Antioch University/Los Angeles. Her work has appeared in *Eunoia Review, Anti-Heroin Chic, San Antonio Review, Drizzle Review, EcoTheo Review,* and *Tupelo Quarterly.* She is an alumna of the Napa Valley Writers' Conference, Idyllwild Writer's Week and is collaborating with a Portland, Oregon composer to set a tanka series.

Kean is the Assistant Dean for Development at USC Gould School of Law and lives in Pasadena, California with her husband of 40 years. They are the proud parents of two grown daughters, whose stories are theirs to share.

margaretannekeanpoet.com

www.ingramcontent.com/pod-product-compliance
Lightning Source LLC
Chambersburg PA
CBHW031206160426
43193CB00008B/529